The Adventures of Murphy and Me

When a Rescue Dog Finds His Forever Home

Written By
Becki A. Jacobson

Publisher: Becki Originals Publishing

ISBN: 978-0578359571

Printed in the U.S.A.

DEDICATION

Dedicated to my mother and my brother who are my warriors. To my father. To Meme, Pepe, and Uncle Gene who encouraged me to share my stories and supplied me with reams of paper and writing utensils. To Murphy who changed my heart and inspires me each day.

Murphy

Do you have a rescue dog?
I do!
His name is Murphy.
Let me share him with you.

Murphy

We walk on the beach
when it is hot.
We even have our own
picnic spot.

He catches the ball
when we play outside.
Sometimes together
we take a car ride.

Murphy

He makes me laugh when
I tickle his tummy.
He loves dog treats because
they are yummy.

He plays with his friends
at the dog park.
He greets people with a smile
instead of a bark.

We watch football together
and our bond is strong.
His tail is fluffy
and super long.

Murphy

He loves the mud
and the snow.
Sometimes I give him
three baths in a row!

Murphy's food

He always spits his food
on the floor.
And when he does,he begs
for more.

He is my rescue puppy
who I brought home to stay.
Together we
sail, laugh, and play.

Murphy is my pup and
my best friend.
We will always share
Love — FOREVER!

Murphy

THE END!

Murphy

THANK YOU FOR READING MY BOOK!

If you enjoyed this book, it would be wonderful if you could take a short minute to leave a lovely review on Amazon, as your kind feedback is very appreciated and so important. It gives me, the author, encouragement for bad days when I want to give up and make balloon animals instead.

Thank you so very much for your time!

~ Becki

About the Author

Becki A. Jacobson grew up in Canterbury, Connecticut. She went to law school and practiced law as a solo practitioner representing clients internationally and throughout the United States. Today, she lives on the coast in Mystic, Connecticut, still practices law, continues to write, and enjoys many adventures with her rescue dog, Murphy.

You may contact her or follow her blog that describes the daily lives of Murphy and Me online at: www.murphyandmeoriginals.com.

Made in the USA
Middletown, DE
12 May 2022

65670566R00018